199 BIBLE PEOPLE, PLACES, AND THINGS

199 BIBLE PEOPLE, PLACES, AND THINGS

Jean Fischer

BARBOUR
PUBLISHING

Published by Barbour Publishing, Inc., P.O. Box 719, Uhrichsville, Ohio 44683 www.barbourbooks.com

Our mission is to publish and distribute inspirational products offering exceptional value and biblical encouragement to the masses.

Member of the Evangelical Christian Publishers Association

Printed in the United States of America.

Contents

INTRODUCTION

The Bible is a big book—actually, a collection of books. Under one cover, you'll find 66 separate books, totaling 1,189 chapters and hundreds of thousands of words. You know the Bible's important, but it can be a bit daunting. That's why we created *199 Bible People, Places, and Things*.

In this little book, you'll find brief, easy-to-read definitions or descriptions of some of the most important names and words in scripture. From Aaron and Abraham through Yahweh, Worship, and Zacchaeus, here are the basic details to help you understand each one. And, if you'd like to study further, we've included plenty of Bible references.

We hope you enjoy this brief survey of 199 of the Bible's most important words and names. As you get to know your Bible better, you'll also gain understanding of the great God who gave you the Bible—the God who made you, keeps you, and offers you salvation.

❶ AARON

MOSES' OLDER BROTHER. Moses wasn't a good speaker, so God told Aaron to speak for him. Moses was the leader and Aaron his spokesman. Aaron helped Moses lead the Hebrew slaves out of Egypt (Exodus 7–12), and God chose Aaron to be Israel's first high priest. He wasn't perfect: When the people asked him to make a statue of a god they could worship, Aaron agreed and fashioned a golden calf (Exodus 32:1–4). God forgave Aaron after Moses prayed for him. Neither Aaron nor Moses made it to the Promised Land because they disobeyed God at a place called Meribah. They were supposed to speak to a rock to create miracle water in the desert—but Moses was angry with the people and hit the rock with a stick instead (Numbers 20:6–12).

❷ ABRAHAM

A MAN OF GREAT FAITH. Abraham and his wife, Sarah, had a son named Isaac, for whom they'd waited for years. But when God decided to test Abraham's faith, He asked the old man to offer Isaac as a sacrifice (Genesis 22:1–13). Abraham was about to do what God asked when the angel of the LORD appeared, saying, "Don't hurt the boy!" (Genesis 22:12 CEV). God had evidence that Abraham would do anything for Him, and the Lord provided another sacrifice—a ram caught in a bush. The apostle Paul called Abraham "the father of us all" (Romans 4:16), the people who come to God through faith in Jesus Christ.

❸ ADAM

THE FIRST PERSON ON EARTH. Adam was good and intelligent (Genesis 2:19–20), but he wasn't perfect—because he disobeyed God's one rule and ate the fruit of a tree God had said to stay away from. Adam was the first worker (Genesis 2:8, 15) and the first husband. God made a woman named Eve to be Adam's wife (Genesis 2:18–25). Their home was the Garden of Eden, but when Adam and Eve sinned, God sent them away from their perfect home forever (Genesis 3:22–24).

➍ ADOPTION

To take someone into your family and make them your own. Children are not always born into the family they grow up in. Instead, they are chosen by nonbiological parents who love them. The apostle Paul talked about a spiritual adoption (Romans 11:1–32; Galatians 4:4–7), saying that anyone can be adopted as God's child if he or she has faith in Jesus Christ (Galatians 3:24–26).

➎ ADVOCATE

A person who supports someone or something. People who speak up or do something for a cause they believe in are called advocates. In many ways, an advocate is a helper. The Bible says that Jesus is our Advocate: "If you. . .sin, Jesus Christ always does the right thing, and he will speak to the Father for us" (1 John 2:1 CEV).

❻ ALPHA AND OMEGA

A TERM THAT MEANS THE BEGINNING AND THE ENDING. In the Greek alphabet, Alpha is the first letter and Omega the last. They remind us that God the Father, His Son Jesus, and the Holy Spirit are here forever and ever. Jesus promised that when He said, "I am the Alpha and the Omega, the Beginning and the End. . .who is and who was and who is to come, the Almighty" (Revelation 1:8 NKJV).

❼ ANDREW

ONE OF JESUS' DISCIPLES, ALSO PETER'S BROTHER. Andrew was a fisherman from the town of Bethsaida (John 1:44). He was a follower of John the Baptist (John 1:35–40), and he introduced Peter to Jesus (John 1:41–42). Andrew was the disciple who brought to Jesus a boy with five loaves of bread and two fishes. Jesus used that small lunch to feed more than five thousand people (John 6:1–14).

❽ ANGEL OF THE LORD

A SPECIAL ANGEL WHO SERVES AS GOD'S SPOKESMAN. He was around a lot in Old Testament times: He appeared to Abraham when he was about to sacrifice his son Isaac (Genesis 22:12), to Hagar in the wilderness (Genesis 16:7–12), and to Moses in the burning bush (Exodus 3:2–3). He also appeared to Gideon (Judges 6:11–12), Balaam (Numbers 22:21–35), Elijah (2 Kings 1:3), David (1 Chronicles 21:16), and others.

❾ ANTICHRIST

SOMEONE WHO IS AGAINST JESUS. Many believe an antichrist will appear at the end of time as the enemy of Christ and all Christians. Another name for this antichrist is the beast (Revelation 13). He will say that Jesus is not the Christ (1 John 2:22–23) and boastfully go against everything holy. He will even sit on God's throne and pretend to be God (2 Thessalonians 2:3–4). In the end, the antichrist will die: "The Lord Jesus will kill him simply by breathing on him" (2 Thessalonians 2:8 CEV).

❿ ARK OF THE COVENANT

A GOLD-PLATED WOODEN CHEST CONTAINING THE TEN COMMANDMENTS. The Ten Commandments were carved on two stone tablets (Exodus 34:28; Deuteronomy 10:3–4), and God said to put them into the ark of the covenant. The New Testament book of Hebrews talks about some manna and Aaron's rod also being in the ark (9:4). God wanted the manna to be placed before the ark (Exodus 16:32–34) to remind the people that He took care of them in the wilderness. Aaron's rod was a sign to those who rebelled against the Lord (Numbers 17:10). God gave detailed instructions for making the ark (Exodus 25:10–22), and when it was done, it was a holy symbol, showing that God was with His people (Exodus 25:22). At first, the ark was stored in the Tabernacle (Exodus 26:33). When the Israelites foolishly took it into battle (1 Samuel 4:1–5), the Philistines captured it (1 Samuel 4:10–11). The Philistines were afflicted while they had the ark, and returned it—later, it was kept in the temple in Jerusalem (1 Kings 8:1–9). King Nebuchadnezzar of Babylon might have stolen it from there (2 Chronicles 36:7, 18), though no one knows for sure what happened to it.

⑪ ASCENSION OF CHRIST

JESUS' RETURN TO HEAVEN AFTER HE ROSE FROM THE DEAD. Jesus was crucified, then buried in a tomb. Three days later, He came to life again and stayed on earth for forty days (Luke 24:1–49; Acts 1:3). After that, He ascended into heaven to be with God (Luke 24:50–51). Jesus' ascension happened at the Mount of Olives, and His disciples were there to see it. "While they were watching, he was taken up into a cloud. They could not see him, but as he went up, they kept looking up into the sky. Suddenly two men dressed in white clothes were standing there beside them. They said, 'Why are you men from Galilee standing here and looking up into the sky? Jesus has been taken to heaven. But he will come back in the same way that you have seen him go'" (Acts 1:9–11 CEV).

❶❷ ATONEMENT

SETTLING DIFFERENCES BETWEEN GOD AND MAN THROUGH A SACRIFICE. In Old Testament times, *atonement* required making animal sacrifices to God. But when Jesus died on the cross, He became the ultimate sacrifice to God. He died so that everyone who believed in Him could be forgiven for their sins (2 Corinthians 5:21). Christ's atonement—the work He did on the cross—is our foundation for peace (Ephesians 2:13–16).

❶❸ BAAL

THE PRIMARY (FALSE) GOD OF THE CANAANITES. They believed Baal made crops grow and livestock reproduce. Sadly, some of God's people worshipped Baal, too, breaking the Second Commandment (Exodus 20:4–5). God sent His prophet Elijah to prove there was only one true God, in a dramatic encounter on Mount Carmel. Many of the people turned from their evil ways, but the rest of them were killed. Read the whole story in 1 Kings 18:1–40.

➊➍ BAPTISM

A CHRISTIAN CEREMONY OF FAITH WHERE PEOPLE ARE DIPPED IN WATER, OR WATER IS POURED OR SPRINKLED ON THEIR HEADS. The ceremony shows our faith in Jesus Christ publicly, and is a symbol of the washing away of our sins. *Baptize* comes from the Greek word *baptizo*, meaning to dunk, dip, or plunge. The New Testament character John the Baptist baptized many people, including Jesus (Matthew 3:4–17). Since Jesus had no sin, He didn't need to be baptized—but He did it to set an example for us (Matthew 3:15).

❶❺ BARABBAS

A NOTORIOUS CRIMINAL. Barabbas was already in jail when Jesus was arrested, imprisoned for sedition and murder. When Jesus was brought to Pontius Pilate, the Roman governor of Judea, to be judged, a mob began shouting for the release of Barabbas. Pilate gave in to their demand: Barabbas was set free, and Jesus was sent to be crucified (Mark 15:6–15).

❶❻ BARNABAS

A FRIEND AND COWORKER OF THE APOSTLE PAUL. Barnabas's real name was Joses, but the apostles called him *Barnabas*, meaning "one who encourages others" (Acts 4:36 CEV). It was Barnabas who convinced the disciples that Paul—once a violent persecutor of Christians—had truly met Jesus on the road to Damascus. In time, Paul became one of Christianity's greatest influences, making multiple missionary journeys and writing a large portion of the New Testament.

❶❼ BATHSHEBA

SOLOMON'S MOTHER. King David saw Bathsheba bathing outdoors, and thought she was beautiful. But she was also married—to Uriah, a soldier in David's army. David called her to his palace, slept with her, and got her pregnant. Then he compounded his sin by making sure that Uriah was killed fighting in a battle (2 Samuel 11:14–17). Once Uriah was dead, David married Bathsheba, who ultimately bore him four sons. One of them was Solomon (2 Samuel 12:24), David's successor as king of Israel.

❶❽ BEATITUDES

B LESSINGS. When Jesus gave the Sermon on the Mount, He blessed the people, in statements now called the Beatitudes. Jesus said, "Blessed are the poor in spirit, for theirs is the kingdom of heaven. Blessed are those who mourn, for they will be comforted. Blessed are the meek, for they will inherit the earth. Blessed are those who hunger and thirst for righteousness, for they will be filled. Blessed are the merciful, for they will be shown mercy. Blessed are the pure in heart, for they will see God. Blessed are the peacemakers, for they will be called sons of God. Blessed are those who are persecuted because of righteousness, for theirs is the kingdom of heaven. Blessed are you when people insult you, persecute you and falsely say all kinds of evil against you because of me. Rejoice and be glad, because great is your reward in heaven" (Matthew 5:3–12 NIV).

❶❾ BENJAMIN

J OSEPH'S LITTLE BROTHER, THE YOUNGEST OF
TWELVE BROTHERS. Their father was Jacob,
and Benjamin and Joseph were dad's favorites
(Genesis 37:3; 42:38) because they were the
sons of Rachel, the wife Jacob loved the most
(Genesis 29:30; 35:24). Benjamin's brothers
were jealous of Joseph, so they sold him as a
slave to merchants who carried him to Egypt
(Genesis 37:28). Years later, Joseph saw his
brothers again, and he forgave them. He
was especially happy to see his baby brother,
Benjamin. A tribe of Israel descended from
Benjamin, known as the Benjamites (Judges
20:35).

⑳ BETHANY

A VILLAGE AT THE FOOT OF THE MOUNT OF OLIVES (MARK 11:1) NEAR JERUSALEM. Jesus went to Bethany often. His good friends Mary, Martha, and Lazarus lived there (John 11:1), and it was in Bethany that Jesus brought Lazarus back to life after he had been dead for four days (John 11:17–44). After Jesus Himself died and came back to life, He ascended into heaven from Bethany (Luke 24:50–51).

㉑ BETHLEHEM

THE PLACE WHERE JESUS WAS BORN. Jesus' earthly parents, Mary and Joseph, were from Nazareth—but they traveled to Bethlehem for a census since that was Joseph's ancestral hometown. When they arrived, Jesus was born (Luke 2:1–11). Bethlehem is also where King David grew up (1 Samuel 16:1–13), and is sometimes called "the city of David" (Luke 2:4).

㉒ BIRTHRIGHT

WEALTH FOR AN OLDEST SON. In Bible times, the oldest son was often given many good things. For example, he would get a double share of everything his father owned when his dad died (Deuteronomy 21:17). Then he would take over as the leader of the family. If the son behaved badly, though, his birthright could be taken away. One son who didn't respect his birthright was Esau, who sold the valuable blessing to his younger brother, Jacob, for a single bowl of stew (Genesis 25:29–34)!

❷❸ BLOOD

The life-sustaining fluid of the body. In Old Testament times, when a person sinned, he killed a healthy, unblemished animal as a sacrifice. The animal's blood was a symbol of the person's blood, or life (Leviticus 17:11). The person didn't have to die for that sin, because the animal took his place. In New Testament times, Jesus sacrificed His own blood and life to pay for *our* sins (Hebrews 9:14). Jesus is sometimes called the "Lamb of God," since He was a perfect sacrifice in every way (1 Peter 1:18–19). Today, when people take communion, they remember that Jesus gave His blood and His life so that God would forgive us for our sins (1 Corinthians 11:25).

㉔ BODY OF CHRIST

ANOTHER NAME FOR CHRIST'S CHURCH.
The apostle Paul called the church
Christ's body (Colossians 1:24). Jesus' Spirit
is always in His body, the church. He rules
over it, and is the head of everything in it
(Ephesians 1:22–23). Every true believer
in any church anywhere in the world is a
member of the body of Christ. The Bible
says that the members of the body of Christ
should help and care for one another (1
Corinthians 12:25–27).

㉕ BOOK OF THE LAW

THE LAW ACCORDING TO MOSES. "The
Book of the Law" is a name for the
first five books of the Old Testament—
Genesis, Exodus, Leviticus, Numbers, and
Deuteronomy—also called the *Pentateuch*.
God gave these laws to Moses, who wrote
them down. Then Moses gave them to the
priests, who read the laws to the people
(Deuteronomy 31:9–11).

❷❻ BRASS SERPENT

A METAL SNAKE GOD USED TO HEAL PEOPLE BITTEN BY REAL SNAKES. Some of the Israelites became so disrespectful of God that He sent poisonous snakes to bite them (Numbers 21:4–6). The people begged Moses for help, and God told Moses to make a snake out of brass and put it on top of a pole. Anyone who was bitten should look at the snake and they would be healed (Numbers 21:7–9). Jesus compared Himself to the brass serpent in John 3:14–15.

㉗ BURNT OFFERING

A GIFT FOR GOD. In Old Testament days, people killed a healthy, unblemished animal, then put parts of the dead animal— its fat, the lower part of its liver, and its two kidneys—on an altar. These parts were burned in a holy ceremony before God (Leviticus 7:1–8).

㉘ CAIN

THE OLDEST SON OF ADAM AND EVE. Cain was jealous because his younger brother Abel's offerings pleased God. Apparently, Cain didn't give the Lord what He really wanted. Before long, Cain's jealousy led to anger, and he took Abel out into a field and killed him. God punished Cain by sending him away (Genesis 4:3–11), making him a "restless wanderer on the earth" (Genesis 4:12 NIV).

㉙ CALVARY

THE HILL WHERE JESUS WAS CRUCIFIED
(JOHN 19:16–17). The word *Calvary*
comes from a Latin word that means "skull."
That is why Calvary is sometimes called
"the Skull." It's also called "Golgotha" (Mark
15:22). The hill was just outside the city
walls of ancient Jerusalem (Luke 23:33). If
you go to Jerusalem today, you can visit the
place where some say Jesus was crucified. The
Church of the Holy Sepulchre marks the site.

㉚ CANAAN

THE PROMISED LAND. Canaan was mainly between the Mediterranean Sea and the Jordan River. Today, this area is Israel, the West Bank, the Gaza Strip, and parts of Lebanon and Syria. Canaan was named after Noah's grandson, Canaan (Genesis 10:1, 6–20). His ancestors, known as the Canaanites, lived on the land for many years. But God promised the land of Canaan to Abraham's ancestors (Genesis 15:3–7). That promise was made true when Joshua led the Israelites to take the land away from the Canaanites (Joshua 10–12).

㉛ CAPERNAUM

A CITY ON THE SHORE OF THE SEA OF GALILEE. Capernaum was Jesus' home during His ministry (Matthew 4:13). His disciples Andrew, Peter, and Philip moved from their hometown of Bethsaida (John 1:44) to Capernaum where disciples Matthew, James, and John lived. All of these men, except Matthew the tax collector, were fishermen (Matthew 4:18–22; 9:9). Jesus sometimes taught in the synagogue there (Mark 1:21), and did many miracles in Capernaum, including healing people and casting out demons (Matthew 8:5–17). Although the people of Capernaum saw His miracles, they did not believe in Him. Jesus scolded them for not having faith (Matthew 11:23–24).

❸❷ CENTURION

A ROMAN SOLDIER. Centurions (Acts 10:1, 22) were military officers commanding a group of about a hundred men. There was a centurion at the foot of the cross when Jesus died. The Bible says, "With a loud cry, Jesus breathed his last. The curtain of the temple was torn in two from top to bottom. And when the centurion, who stood there in front of Jesus, heard his cry and saw how he died, he said, 'Surely this man was the Son of God!'" (Mark 15:37–39 NIV).

㉝ Cherubim

Heavenly winged creatures. After God sent Adam and Eve from the Garden of Eden, the cherubim showed up. They guarded the entrance so Adam and Eve couldn't return (Genesis 3:24). Ezekiel saw cherubim, too: "Each of the winged creatures had four faces: the face of a bull, the face of a human, the face of a lion, and the face of an eagle" (Ezekiel 10:14 CEV). The ark of the covenant had golden cherubim statues on its lid (Exodus 25:18–20).

㉞ Circumcision

A RELIGIOUS CEREMONY PERFORMED ON BOYS. Circumcision was a symbol of God's agreement with the Israelites (Genesis 17:3–14). Israelite boys were circumcised eight days after they were born (Leviticus 12:3). The word has another meaning, too. In the New Testament, *circumcision* can mean putting off sin (Colossians 2:11).

㉟ Comforter

A NOTHER NAME FOR THE HOLY SPIRIT. The Comforter, or Holy Spirit, is our Helper. Jesus said, "I will ask the Father, and He will give you another Helper, that He may be with you forever" (John 14:16 NASB). The Holy Spirit teaches us and gives us advice, reminding us of what Jesus would do (John 14:26).

❸❻ CONDEMNATION

T HE PUNISHMENT FOR BEING GUILTY OF SIN. Everyone is guilty of sin, but Christ died so we could be forgiven (Romans 5:8). If Jesus hadn't come, we would all be condemned—no one would ever get to heaven. But Jesus came to save us from condemnation (John 3:17–18). If we truly believe in Jesus, we will live with Him forever in glory.

37 CORINTH

A COASTAL CITY NEAR ATHENS, GREECE. Corinth was known for how badly its people behaved. The apostle Paul lived in Corinth for eighteen months. He taught there, and tried to convince people to believe in Jesus. Many of the people believed and were baptized (Acts 18:1–11).

38 CORNELIUS

O NE OF THE FIRST GENTILES TO BECOME A CHRISTIAN. Cornelius was a Roman soldier, and Jews weren't supposed to interact with Gentiles like him. But Cornelius loved God, who told him to call for the apostle Peter. The Holy Spirit told Peter to accept Cornelius as a Christian. After that, other Gentiles became Christians and were baptized. Read more in Acts 10.

❸❾ COVENANT

AN AGREEMENT OR PROMISE. God often made covenants with His people, promising to bless them if they obeyed and followed Him (Genesis 22:15–18). God made a covenant with Noah after the flood, saying, "Never again will all life be cut off by the waters of a flood; never again will there be a flood to destroy the earth" (Genesis 9:11 NIV). God put a rainbow in the sky as a symbol of His covenant (Genesis 9:12–17). Jesus said that His blood was a covenant (Matthew 26:28), promising that those who believe in Him would be saved from condemnation (John 10:9).

40 CROSS

WHAT JESUS DIED ON. The cross was made out of two heavy wooden posts, with a long piece stuck into the ground and a shorter crosspiece toward the top. Jesus needed help to carry His cross to the place where He was crucified (Matthew 27:32). There, His hands and feet were nailed to the cross, its long post was set upright in the ground, and He was left hanging there to die (Luke 23:33). Jesus was on the cross six hours before He died (John 19:30–33). Today, we remember that event on Good Friday.

4️⃣1️⃣ CUBIT

AN ANCIENT MEASUREMENT. A cubit was the length from a man's elbow to the tip of his middle finger—about 18 inches. Noah's ark was 300 cubits long, 50 cubits wide, and 30 cubits high. That comes out to about 450 feet long, 75 feet wide, and 45 feet high (Genesis 6:15).

4️⃣2️⃣ DAMASCUS

THE CAPITAL CITY OF SYRIA, NORTHEAST OF JERUSALEM. Damascus is one of the world's oldest cities, and is mentioned often in the Bible—as far back as the book of Genesis (14:15). It was near Damascus that the persecutor Saul, later known as Paul, became a Christian (Acts 9:1–25).

❹❸ DANIEL

A N OLD TESTAMENT PROPHET. Daniel was loyal to God in a time when many people worshipped false gods. God gave Daniel the gift of explaining people's dreams (Daniel 4), which sometimes predicted things that would happen in the future. Daniel is well known for being thrown into a den of lions for refusing to pray to King Darius. But God sent an angel to watch over Daniel, shutting the lions' mouths so they wouldn't eat him. Read the whole story in Daniel 6:1–24.

➍➍ DAVID

THE MOST PROMINENT KING OF ISRAEL.
David was an ancestor of Jesus (Luke
2:4–7), and like Jesus, he was born in
Bethlehem (1 Samuel 17:12). As a young
man, David used a sling to fight a Philistine
giant named Goliath (1 Samuel 17:20–52).
David was a shepherd and later a musician
for King Saul (1 Samuel 16:14–21). Later,
when God deposed Saul for his bad behavior,
David was made the new king (1 Samuel
16:11–13). He was a very successful warrior
(2 Samuel 8:1–15), and he wrote many of the
psalms in the Bible.

45 DEAD SEA

A LAKE IN ISRAEL NEAR JERUSALEM. It is about fifty miles long by ten miles wide. Also known as the Sea of Salt, the lake's water is so salty that very few creatures can live in it. But the prophet Ezekiel saw a vision of a new Dead Sea, full of fresh water and many kinds of fish. The land around it will be lush and green because the water is good (Ezekiel 47:6–12).

46 DEBORAH

A JUDGE AND PROPHETESS. Deborah was a very powerful woman in Israel. She was also a military leader, as with her army's general, Barak, she battled the Canaanites and won (Judges 4:4–24). Afterward, she and Barak praised God with a song recorded in Judges 5.

❹❼ DELILAH

SAMSON'S PHILISTINE GIRLFRIEND. **Delilah** was the woman who had Samson's long hair cut off. (He was sleeping when that happened.) Since, by God's design, Samson's hair gave him strength, he became very weak without it. Soon he was captured by his Philistine enemies (Judges 16:13–21).

❹❽ DEVIL

SATAN HIMSELF. The devil wants to get people to do wrong things. He even tempted Jesus (Matthew 4:1–11), though of course, he got nowhere. Jesus is much more powerful than the devil, and wasn't fooled by his tricks. Jesus called the devil a murderer and a liar, even "the father of lies" (John 8:44). With God's help, Christians stand up to the devil's evil (Ephesians 6:10–12).

㊾ DISCIPLE

ONE WHO FOLLOWS JESUS. The original twelve disciples were Peter, Andrew, James the son of Zebedee, John, Philip, Bartholomew, Thomas, Matthew, James the son of Alphaeus, Thaddaeus, Simon, and Judas (Matthew 10:2–4). It was the disciples' job to spread the gospel of Jesus Christ (John 15:16). Jesus gave His disciples the power to cast out evil spirits and to heal the sick (Matthew 10:1). Today, a disciple of Jesus is anyone who follows His teachings.

50 DOCTRINE

A SET OF IDEAS. Jesus taught about God and living the right way. Paul, Peter, and other Bible writers added to Jesus' teaching. All of their thoughts make up the Christian *doctrine*. Over the years, this doctrine has spread all over the world as people believed and became Christians.

51 EGYPT

A COUNTRY IN NORTHERN AFRICA ON THE NILE RIVER. Many key Bible events took place in Egypt. Abram went there during a famine in Canaan (Genesis 12:10). Jacob's family lived in Egypt (Genesis 46:6). His ancestors became the Hebrew nation. The Hebrew people were held as slaves in Egypt for four hundred years. God told Moses to go and set them free (Exodus 3:7–10). In New Testament times, after Jesus was born, King Herod wanted Him killed—so an angel told Mary and Joseph to take Jesus to Egypt and hide (Matthew 2:13–14). Today, Egypt is a major country in Africa with a population of almost eighty million.

52 ELECT

SPECIAL ONES CHOSEN BY GOD. Even before we were born, God decided whether we would believe in Him and be saved (Romans 8:29). The Bible says that God wants everyone to be saved (2 Peter 3:9), but those who refuse to believe in Jesus will be lost (John 5:39–40)—they will not go to heaven. God's chosen people should try to behave like Jesus (Romans 8:29). They should love God, love others, and live according to His rules.

53 ELIJAH

An Old Testament prophet. God told Elijah to give a message to the wicked king Ahab. The message was that no rain would fall on the king's land for three years (1 Kings 17:1). Ahab was angry, and he took it out on Elijah—so God told Elijah to hide near the Jordan River (1 Kings 17:5). There, God sent ravens to feed the prophet, who received bread and meat every day (1 Kings 17:6). Later, Elijah had a contest with King Ahab, pitting the one true God against Ahab's false god Baal, which, of course, God won (1 Kings 18:16–39). At the end of his life on earth, Elijah was taken to heaven in a very special way, as God sent a chariot and horses of fire which carried Elijah off in a whirlwind (2 Kings 2:11).

54 ELISABETH

ZACHARIAS'S WIFE AND JOHN THE BAPTIST'S MOTHER. Elisabeth was a relative of Jesus' mother, Mary. Both women were expecting babies at the same time. They knew their babies were special, because angels from the Lord had told them so (Matthew 1:20–21; Luke 1:11–13). Both women believed that the baby inside Mary was the Messiah and Savior, and they celebrated together that Jesus would soon be born (Luke 1:39–55). Elisabeth had her baby, John, first; then Jesus was born about six months later.

55 ELISHA

AN OLD TESTAMENT PROPHET. Since Elisha was the prophet Elijah's assistant, he was there to see Elijah disappear in a whirlwind. Elisha took Elijah's place as leader of the prophets (2 Kings 2:15), serving under four kings and performing numerous miracles.

56 ENOCH

A GREAT-GRANDFATHER OF NOAH (GENESIS 5:22–29). Enoch was the first son of Cain, and also the name of a city, as Cain built the city and named it after his son (Genesis 4:17). Enoch lived 365 years (Genesis 5:23), but he didn't die like a normal person. God just took him away (Genesis 5:24). This event, which theologians call "translation," is noted in the New Testament in Hebrews 11:5. It says Enoch was taken away because he was so faithful to God. Enoch had a son named Methuselah, who had the longest life span recorded in the Bible—969 years (Genesis 5:27).

57 EPISTLE

A LETTER. Many of the New Testament books are epistles. Paul wrote fourteen epistles. John wrote three. Peter wrote two. James and Jude each wrote one.

58 ESTHER

QUEEN OF PERSIA. The Old Testament book of Esther tells the story of young Esther—also called Hadassah—a Jewish orphan raised by her cousin Mordecai (Esther 2:7). After a nationwide beauty contest, she became the queen of Persia (Esther 2:17). Esther saved her people, the Jews, from an evil man named Haman, an aide to the Persian king. Because he was angry with Mordecai, Haman planned to kill all the Jews (Esther 3:5–6). When Esther found out about it, she risked her life to request the king's help. In the end, Haman was hanged and the Jews successfully defended themselves from attack.

(59) EUTYCHUS

A YOUNG MAN WHO DIED DURING A SERMON. Sitting in a third-story window while the apostle Paul was preaching, Eutychus fell asleep, dropped to the ground, and died. He was picked up, dead, but Paul put his arms around Eutychus and said, "Don't worry! He's alive" (Acts 20:9–10 CEV). The people were "not a little comforted" (Acts 20:12 KJV).

⑥⓪ EVE

THE FIRST WOMAN. Eve is sometimes called the mother of the human race (Genesis 3:20). God made her from one of Adam's ribs (Genesis 2:21–22) so that Adam would have a helper. They lived in a garden called Eden, with freedom to eat from any tree except one—the tree of the knowledge of good and evil (Genesis 2:17). One day, a serpent—Satan in disguise—approached Eve to tempt her to eat the forbidden fruit. She did, and she also gave some to Adam (Genesis 3:1–6). God was angry that Eve and Adam had disobeyed, and pronounced a curse on the ground. God told Adam and Eve that they would have to work hard for the rest of their lives (Genesis 3:19). Then He sent them out of the garden forever (Genesis 3:23).

(61) EZEKIEL

A PROPHET, PRIEST, AND AUTHOR. God allowed Ezekiel to "see" things that would happen in the future (Ezekiel 1:3). He wrote the Old Testament book called by his name. It predicted things that were to come. Most of Ezekiel's predictions were about Israel and the Jewish people, though some of his predictions have yet to come true. They refer to the end times when Jesus will come back to earth.

(62) FAITH

CONFIDENCE IN SOMETHING YOU'VE BEEN TOLD. *Faith* is another word for trust. It's believing in God, even though you can't see Him (Hebrews 11:1). Like the air we breathe, God can't be seen—but we know by faith they're there. Jesus said anything is possible when we put our faith in God (Mark 9:23). The very first point of faith is this: to believe that Jesus was sent by God to save us from our sins. If we have faith in Him, our souls won't die. Instead, we'll live forever with God (John 3:16).

(63) Fall of Man

When Adam and Eve made a huge mistake by disobeying God. Adam and Eve were the first people on earth, and God gave them just one rule to obey: They could not eat fruit from a particular tree in the Garden of Eden. As created, Adam and Eve knew only good things—but by eating that fruit, they would know the difference between good and evil. The "fall of man" came when Satan got Eve to taste the fruit. She then gave some to Adam, who ate it, too. As punishment, God sent Adam and Eve out of the garden forever (Genesis 3). Since that time, all humans know good from evil and have a choice to obey or disobey God. Sadly, there is not one person on earth who has not disobeyed (Romans 3:23).

(64) FAMINE

A WIDESPREAD LACK OF FOOD. There were many famines in Bible times. Some were caused when there wasn't enough rain. Others were caused by hailstorms (Exodus 9:23), insects (Exodus 10:13–15), and enemies (Deuteronomy 28:49–51). When the Israelites were in the Desert of Sin, they were starving until God made manna appear on the ground (Exodus 16:4).

65 FAST

To stop eating or drinking for a while. Fasting was common in Bible times, and some people still fast today as a way to be close to God. Leaders in Bible times sometimes ordered people to fast (Ezra 8:21). Jesus Himself fasted (Luke 4:1–4), teaching that when people fast, they should do it in secret (Matthew 6:16–18). In other words, fasting should be a private thing between a person and God, not something done for show.

66 FIRMAMENT

The sky. *Firmament* is an Old Testament word for the heavens, or the sky above the earth (Genesis 1:6–8 KJV).

(67) FLOOD, THE

GOD'S DO-OVER IN THE TIME OF NOAH (GENESIS 6–9). After Adam and Eve sinned in the Garden of Eden, human beings went downhill fast. God decided to wipe out the whole earth with a massive flood. Only Noah, seven members of his family, and pairs of certain animals survived in a giant boat Noah built (the ark). When the flood went away—about a year later—the people and animals were to start over and refill the earth with life. God told Noah He would never flood the earth again, and sealed that promise with a rainbow (Genesis 9:13–17).

(68) FOOT-WASHING

WASHING THE FEET OF GUESTS IN YOUR HOME. In Bible times, since people's feet got really dirty on the dry, dusty walking paths, hosts washed their visitors' feet. It was a way of saying, "Welcome to our home." Though servants usually did the foot-washing, Jesus washed His disciples' feet to teach them a lesson: They weren't to think that they were better than anyone else (John 13:1–17).

(69) FORGIVENESS

OVERLOOKING THE WRONG ANOTHER PERSON HAS DONE. Forgiveness can be hard, especially if the offense was a bad one. But Jesus said if we forgive others for the bad things *they* do, God will forgive *us* for the bad things we do (Matthew 6:14–15). Jesus came to earth to take the punishment for our sins (Acts 10:43)—God's forgiveness for those who ask Him. As forgiven people, we can ask God to help us forgive others (Matthew 6:12).

⑦⓪ GABRIEL

AN IMPORTANT ANGEL (LUKE 1:19).
Gabriel brought messages from God,
and appeared a few times in the Bible. The
prophet Daniel saw him twice. Gabriel
helped him understand his dreams (Daniel
8:15–17; Daniel 9:21–24). Gabriel appeared
to Zechariah, too, telling him that his son
would grow up to be John the Baptist (Luke
1:11–19). And Gabriel appeared to Mary,
Jesus' mother, saying that she would give birth
to Jesus, the Son of God (Luke 1:26–45).

71 GARDEN OF EDEN

ADAM'S AND EVE'S FIRST HOME. A river flowed through the garden, splitting into four other rivers: the Pishon and Gihon (which no longer exist) and the Tigris and Euphrates. The garden had many trees, but there was one particular tree Adam and Eve could not eat from—the "tree of the knowledge of good and evil" (Genesis 2:9). When they broke God's rule and ate fruit from the forbidden tree, they brought sin and death into the world (Romans 5:12). God made them leave the garden forever (Genesis 3).

🅐🅑 GENTILES

PEOPLE WHO ARE NOT OF THE JEWISH RACE. In Bible times, Jews looked down on Gentiles, viewing them as "unclean." In fact, it was against the law for a Jew to even visit a Gentile (Acts 10:28). But Jesus changed that. His death and resurrection allowed *everyone* to be forgiven for their sins, if they ask (Galatians 3:28). When the Gentiles first heard that Jesus died for their sins, too, they were very glad (Acts 13:46–48).

❼❸ GETHSEMANE

A GARDEN OUTSIDE JERUSALEM. The Garden of Gethsemane is a famous place near the Mount of Olives. Jesus prayed there the night He was arrested. Earlier, as Jesus ate supper with His disciples, He told them He was about to be arrested and killed. When He went into the Garden of Gethsemane to pray, He was very sad (Mark 14:33–34), saying to God, "My Father, if it is possible, don't make me suffer by having me drink from this cup. But do what you want, and not what I want" (Matthew 26:39 CEV). A short time later, Jesus was arrested and taken away (John 18:1–12).

𝟳𝟰 GIDEON

A FAITHFUL HERO OF THE OLD TESTAMENT
(HEBREWS 11:32–34). Gideon was a
leader in Israel, called by God to fight the
powerful Midianite army (Judges 6:14–16)
which God had been using to punish Israel
for its sins (Judges 6:1). When Gideon and
his servants destroyed an altar to the false
god Baal, replacing it with one to honor God
(Judges 6:25–27), the Midianites were moved
to attack. They came after Gideon with a
huge army, "thick as locusts" (Judges 7:12
NIV). Gideon had more than thirty thousand
men in his army, but God narrowed that
group down to just three hundred, to show
the Israelites that they shouldn't trust in
their own power. With that tiny army—and
God's intervention—Gideon defeated the
Midianites (Judges 7:16–25).

75 GLEANING

GATHERING LEFTOVER CROPS. The Bible describes harvesters who went into fields to pick grain, and the poor people who were allowed to follow them to collect the leftovers (Leviticus 19:9–10). In the Bible story of Ruth, she was gleaning barley and wheat from a field that belonged to a man named Boaz (Ruth 2).

❼❻ GOD

THE CREATOR AND RULER OF THE UNIVERSE
(ISAIAH 40:28). God is the ultimate
reality (Isaiah 40:18). He can do anything
and everything (Jeremiah 32:17). God is our
heavenly Father (Matthew 6:9), who knows
all our weaknesses (Psalm 103:14), thoughts
(Psalm 44:21), and words (Psalm 139:4). He
knows our actions (Psalm 139:2) and our
needs (Matthew 6:32). God is so great that
He is everywhere at the same time (Jeremiah
23:23–24). He is more powerful than
anything else (Revelation 19:6), yet forgiving,
wise, and truthful (Psalm 136; Colossians
2:2–3; Titus 1:2). God loved people so much
that He sent His Son Jesus to earth to save us
from our sins. He promised that if we believe
in Jesus, our souls will live forever with Him
(John 3:16).

77 GOLDEN CALF

AN IDOL AARON MADE. In Bible times, people created false gods and worshipped them, making the true God angry. Aaron, Moses' brother, foolishly made a golden calf for the Israelites. He was waiting with the people while Moses was on the mountain with God, receiving the Ten Commandments. When Moses was away for a long time, the people lost faith and asked Aaron to make a god to lead them. Aaron fashioned a golden calf out of the Israelites' jewelry. The people bowed down and worshipped the statue, infuriating God. Read the whole story in Exodus 32.

❼❽ GOLIATH

A GIANT MORE THAN NINE FEET TALL.
Goliath was a Philistine warrior from the
city of Gath. He fought with the Philistine
army in a great war with the Israelites.
Every day, Goliath dared the Israelites to
choose a soldier to fight him one-on-one,
but no Jewish soldier wanted to. "He wore
a bronze helmet and had bronze armor to
protect his chest and legs. The chest armor
alone weighed about one hundred twenty-
five pounds. He carried a bronze sword
strapped on his back, and his spear was so
big that the iron spearhead alone weighed
more than fifteen pounds" (1 Samuel 17:5–7
CEV). But David, a brave young shepherd boy,
volunteered to fight Goliath—and with just
a slingshot and a stone, he killed the giant.
Read more in 1 Samuel 17.

79 GOSPEL

THE "GOOD NEWS" (MARK 1:15); NAMELY, THAT JESUS DIED SO WE CAN LIVE FOREVER! God sent His Son, Jesus, into the world to live among the people. While He was here, Jesus taught about God. Then He died on a cross as a sacrifice for sin, and three days later rose from the dead to prove His power over death (Luke 24:3–8). Jesus promised that whoever believes in Him will not die, but will live forever with God (John 3:16).

80 GRACE

GOD'S FAVOR THAT WE DON'T DESERVE.
Our sins offend God. But grace is
given to those who believe in Jesus (Titus
2:11). There is no way humans can be perfect
like God. Everyone sins (1 John 1:8). After
Adam and Eve disobeyed God, humans were
punished for their sins. In the Old Testament,
people had to sacrifice animals to become
right with God. But Jesus changed that by
dying on the cross (Romans 4:25). He took
the blame for the bad things we do—and if
we believe in Jesus, by the grace of God we
are saved (Ephesians 2:4–6). Grace is a gift
from God (Ephesians 2:8).

81 HANNAH

THE PROPHET SAMUEL'S MOTHER. Hannah was barren, but when she asked God for a son, He said yes. Hannah promised God that her son would be faithful and serve Him, so she allowed the priest Eli to raise Samuel in the tabernacle, where the people of Israel went to worship God. Hannah's beautiful prayer, thanking God for His blessings, is recorded in 1 Samuel 2:1–10.

82 HEAVEN

GOD'S HOME (1 KINGS 8:34). Jesus said He was going to heaven to prepare a place for us. He promised to come back for us so we can be with Him always (John 14:2–3). Heaven is a place of great reward (Matthew 5:12).

(83) Hell

WHERE UNBELIEVERS GO WHEN THEY DIE. Hell is the antithesis of heaven. A terrible place, hell is described as a land of "fire that shall never be quenched" (Mark 9:43 NKJV) and where people are shut away from God and His kindness (2 Thessalonians 1:9).

(84) Heresy

BELIEFS AND TEACHINGS ABOUT GOD AND THE BIBLE THAT AREN'T TRUE. The Bible often uses the phrase "false teachers" to describe people who promote heresy: "But there were false prophets also among the people, even as there shall be false teachers among you, who privily shall bring in damnable heresies, even denying the Lord that bought them, and bring upon themselves swift destruction. And many shall follow their pernicious ways" (2 Peter 2:1–2 KJV).

85 HEZEKIAH

THE TUNNELING KING. Hezekiah was a godly king in Jerusalem, one who stopped his people from worshipping idols. He also took advice from God's prophet Isaiah (Isaiah 38:1–8). When Hezekiah thought the Assyrian army might attack Jerusalem, he worried that he and his people would be trapped inside. So he ordered a tunnel dug through solid rock from the city to a spring outside to carry water into Jerusalem. If they were trapped inside, there would be water to drink (2 Chronicles 32:30). It also left less water for the Assyrians to use (2 Chronicles 32:2–4).

86 HIGH PRIEST

THE LEADER OF THE PRIESTS. Aaron, Moses' older brother, was the first high priest of Israel. When he died, his son, Eleazar, became high priest. This continued through the generations, as all the high priests of Israel were descendants of Aaron (Exodus 28). Jesus Christ is called the "great high priest" (Hebrews 4:14), because He gave His own life as a sacrifice for all people (Hebrews 9:26).

87 HOLY SPIRIT

GOD'S THIRD "PERSON." God is three persons in one: God the Father, Jesus the Son, and the Holy Spirit (Matthew 28:19). The Holy Spirit's purpose is to help and support all the people who believe in God (John 14:12–27). After Jesus died and ascended to heaven, He sent the Holy Spirit to be with His followers (Acts 2:1–21). The Holy Spirit is sometimes called the *Helper*, and one of His jobs is to help people understand what's in the Bible (1 Corinthians 2:13). He's also called the *Comforter* (John 14:16) because He encourages us in hard times. The Holy Spirit can convict nonbelievers of their sin (John 16:8), so they might believe in Jesus and be saved.

88 HOSANNA

A SHOUT OF PRAISE TO GOD. *Hosanna* means "save us now." It's what the crowd shouted when Jesus rode into Jerusalem on a young donkey (Matthew 21:9). Today, we celebrate that day as Palm Sunday.

89 HOSEA

AN OLD TESTAMENT BOOK NAMED FOR THE PROPHET WHO WROTE IT. Hosea preached to the northern kingdom of Israel. God told Hosea that He would allow His people to be punished by their enemies for a while. Then God would save them from the punishment (Hosea 4–14). Hosea is probably best known for marrying a "wife of whoredoms" (Hosea 1:2) at God's command. Their marriage—a faithful husband and an adulterous wife—pictured God's relationship to Israel.

90 I AM

GOD'S SPECIAL NAME FOR HIMSELF. When God spoke to Moses through a burning bush, He called Himself *I AM*. God said, "This is my name forever, the name by which I am to be remembered from generation to generation" (Exodus 3:14–15 NIV). Since God has always existed and will continue forever (Revelation 1:8), He simply *is*. Many people call Jesus "the Great I Am," since He used the words "I am" several times to describe Himself in the Gospel of John (John 6:35, 8:12, 10:7, 10:11, 11:25, 14:6, and 15:5).

⑨① IDOL

ANYTHING WORSHIPPED THAT IS NOT GOD (ROMANS 1:25). In Bible times, there were many instances of idol worship. Many people—even Israelites—worshipped a false god named Baal (Numbers 25:3). Exodus 32 describes Aaron's mistake in making a golden calf for Israel. Other idols were made from different kinds of metal and wood. The first of God's Ten Commandments says: "You shall have no other gods before Me" (Exodus 20:3). Idol worship makes God jealous and angry (Psalm 78:58).

92 INSPIRATION

GOD LEADING PEOPLE TO DO GOOD THINGS. God inspires people in many ways. He "breathed out" (the literal meaning of *inspired*) the content of scripture (2 Timothy 3:16). He spoke to prophets and sent them into the world with His messages (1 Samuel 19:20). A few times, God talked out loud to people (Exodus 3). He also inspired through dreams (Daniel 1:17) and visions (Ezekiel 11:24–25). And He gives wisdom to help us understand today (Job 32:8).

(93) ISAAC

ABRAHAM AND SARAH'S SON. When Isaac was born, his parents were very old—Abraham was a hundred (Genesis 21:5) and Sarah was ninety (Genesis 17:17). When Isaac was a boy, God decided to test Abraham's faith by asking Abraham to offer his son as a sacrifice (Genesis 22:1–2). Abraham was ready to do what God asked when an angel of the Lord appeared. "Don't hurt the boy!" the angel said (Genesis 22:12 CEV). Isaac's life was spared, and he grew up and married a girl named Rebekah (Genesis 25:20). They had twin boys named Jacob and Esau (Genesis 25:23–26), both of whom started great nations—Jacob, the nation of Israel.

94 ISAIAH

An Old Testament prophet. Isaiah worked in the city of Jerusalem, giving messages from God to King Uzziah and the kings who followed him. Isaiah warned that the Assyrians would destroy Jerusalem and Israel, but he added that some of God's people would be saved (Isaiah 1:2–9, 11:11). He predicted King Hezekiah's death, then told the king that God was going to give him fifteen more years to live (2 Kings 20). Isaiah also predicted Jesus' birth (Isaiah 7:14). Isaiah described a man who would tell people to prepare for Jesus (Isaiah 40:3). That man was John the Baptist (Matthew 3:1–3).

95 ISRAEL

A VERY IMPORTANT BIBLE NAME. *Israel* had three usages in scripture. First, it was a new name God gave Jacob, after Jacob wrestled all night with God at a place called Penuel (Genesis 32:24–32). Second, Jacob's twelve sons and all their descendants became a nation called "Israel" after Jacob's new name. Third, a smaller nation of Israel formed in 931 BC when ten tribes split from the twelve tribes of Israel. They created their own nation with its own king, Jeroboam (1 Kings 12), and a capital city of Samaria. This Israel existed for about two hundred years before it was overrun by Assyria in 722 BC (2 Kings 17:23–24).

96 JACOB

THE SON OF ISAAC AND REBEKAH. Jacob and his brother, Esau, were twins. Esau was the older of the two (Genesis 25:24–26), and as the oldest, was promised a special blessing after his father's death. But he sold his right to the fortune to his younger brother, Jacob, for a bowl of stew (Genesis 25:29–34)! Jacob had schemed to steal his father's blessing, and Esau was so angry he decided to kill Jacob (see Genesis 27:1–41). When their mother found out, she sent Jacob to live with an uncle (Genesis 27:42–46). On his way there, Jacob had a dream of a ladder to heaven with angels going up and down. God spoke to Jacob, promising him land and many ancestors. Read more in Genesis 28:10–15. Jacob grew up, got married, and had a large family. God changed Jacob's name to Israel (Genesis 32:28), and all of his ancestors were known as the Israelites. His son Joseph became important in the kingdom of Egypt.

97 JAMES

A DISCIPLE OF JESUS. James lived in Capernaum and worked as a fisherman. He was at the Sea of Galilee when Jesus chose him as a disciple, along with James' younger brother, John (Matthew 4:21). Jesus called the brothers "Sons of Thunder" (Mark 3:17), perhaps because they had strong tempers. James shared many important moments with Jesus: He was there when God appeared to Jesus in a bright cloud, saying, "This is my Son, whom I love; with him I am well pleased" (Matthew 17:5 NIV). James was also present when Jesus brought a dead girl back to life (Luke 8:49–56) and when the Lord was transfigured (Mark 9:2). James was also with Jesus the night He was arrested (Mark 14:33).

98 JEREMIAH

A PROPHET IN OLD TESTAMENT TIMES. God chose Jeremiah even before he was born (Jeremiah 1:4–5). When he grew up, he was sad that the Israelites were behaving so badly (Jeremiah 9:1), and became known as the "weeping prophet." Jeremiah warned the people, saying God would punish them for their behavior (Jeremiah 16:1–21). But the people didn't listen, and even turned against Jeremiah, plotting to kill him (Jeremiah 11:21). Even Jeremiah's family turned on him (Jeremiah 12:6). But God did what He promised through Jeremiah: The Babylonians took over the land, and the people were taken away as prisoners (Jeremiah 27:6).

99 JERICHO

A N ANCIENT WALLED CITY. Jericho was
near the Jordan River and the Dead Sea.
Joshua captured Jericho when the Israelites
entered the Promised Land (Joshua 6:1–
22)—his faith in God made the walls around
the city fall down (Hebrews 11:30)! In New
Testament times, Jesus visited Jericho, where
He taught and healed people. This was where
Jesus gave sight to the blind man, Bartimaeus
(Mark 10:46–52). Jericho was also the place
where Zacchaeus climbed a tree to better see
Jesus (Luke 19:1–9).

(100) JERUSALEM

A FAMOUS CITY, BOTH IN BIBLE TIMES AND TODAY. Jerusalem is an ancient city, the most important city to the Jewish people. Jerusalem existed when the first book of the Bible, Genesis, was written. At that time, it was called Salem (Genesis 14:18). Later known as Jebus (Judges 19:10), Jerusalem gained its current name by the time of the sixth book of the Bible, Joshua (Joshua 10:1). Jerusalem was the site of God's temple (1 Kings 3:1; 6:1–38), and was fought over often. Jesus cried because Jerusalem was sinful (Luke 19:41–42), and rode into the city on a young donkey (Matthew 21:1–11). He was crucified just outside Jerusalem's city walls (Luke 23:33). Someday, God will create a perfect city where there will be no sin, calling it "the new Jerusalem" (Revelation 21:2).

101 JESUS CHRIST

SON OF GOD; SAVIOR OF THE WORLD. Jesus was born in Bethlehem to a young woman named Mary (Luke 2:4–7, 21). His father is God through a miraculous conception in Mary, who was a virgin. Her husband, Joseph, acted as Jesus' father on earth.

When Jesus was born, King Herod was jealous, fearing Jesus would challenge his position. So Herod plotted to kill Jesus. When an angel warned Mary and Joseph, they ran away with Jesus to Egypt, and His life was spared (Matthew 2:13–14).

As a man, Jesus taught crowds of people about God. He chose twelve men—His disciples—to help Him (Matthew 10:1–4). Jesus taught truths about God and His kingdom, healed the sick, and performed many other miracles. The people were amazed at what He could do. Many believed Jesus was the Son of God, though others rejected Him.

The Jewish leaders were jealous of Jesus and wanted Him killed (Matthew 26:3–4). When they saw an opportunity, they arrested Jesus and accused Him of blasphemy for claiming to be God's Son (Mark 14:55–65). Jesus was crucified; then His body was put in a tomb (John 19). Three days later, though, Jesus came back to life and appeared to many people over a period of forty days (Acts 1:3). After one last meeting with His disciples, Jesus ascended to heaven on a cloud (Luke 24:36–51).

Jesus' death was part of God the Father's plan. God sacrificed Jesus, His own Son, to save people from sin (Mark 10:45). When Jesus died, He took all of our sins on Himself; when He came back to life, He proved that He is the Son of God. If we believe in what Jesus did, God will forgive us for our sins (Acts 16:31). Jesus promised to come back to earth someday, to take all who believe in Him to heaven.

(102) JEZEBEL

KING AHAB'S WICKED WIFE. Queen Jezebel persuaded the Israelites to worship the false god Baal, and killed some of God's prophets (1 Kings 18:4). Then, another of God's prophets, Elijah, predicted that Jezebel would be killed. Furious, Jezebel planned to kill Elijah (1 Kings 19:1–2), but he escaped. When a new king, Jehu, came to power, he had Jezebel and her whole family executed (2 Kings 9:30–37). No one from her family ever ruled Israel again.

(103) JOB

A MAN FAMOUS FOR SUFFERING. Job was a very good man (Job 1:1) with a large family and extensive property—in sheep, camels, cows, and servants. When Satan said Job served God only for His blessings, God let Satan attack Job's possessions. First, Job lost his children, animals, and servants. Then, with God's permission, Satan attacked Job's health. But Job refused to "curse God and die," as his wife suggested (Job 2:9). The old phrase "the patience of Job" isn't entirely true, because Job spent a lot of time complaining to God. In the end, though, Job learned that God knows best, even when we suffer. God returned to Job the possessions he'd lost (and more), even giving him ten more children (Job 42).

(104) JOHN

JESUS' CLOSEST FRIEND. John was one of Jesus' twelve disciples. He lived in Capernaum and fished on the shores of the Sea of Galilee. John's father was Zebedee, and his brother, James, another disciple (Matthew 4:21–22). He might have had a temper, since Jesus called John and his brother James "Sons of Thunder" (Mark 3:17). John described himself as "the disciple whom Jesus loved" (John 19:26). After Jesus returned to heaven, John wrote one of the four Gospels. He also wrote three New Testament letters and the book of Revelation.

(105) JOHN THE BAPTIST

A PROPHET WHO PREPARED THE WAY FOR JESUS. The son of Zacharias and Elisabeth, John was also related to Jesus. The Old Testament prophet Isaiah made predictions about John: "Someone is shouting: 'Clear a path in the desert! Make a straight road for the LORD our God' " (Isaiah 40:3 CEV). Some seven hundred years later, those predictions came true as John the Baptist began preaching in the desert (Matthew 3:1–3), preparing the way for Jesus.

John wore clothes made of camel's hair and ate grasshoppers and wild honey. Crowds of people came to him to be baptized in the Jordan River. In fact, John even baptized Jesus, though reluctantly. He didn't think he was worthy to baptize such a great man (Matthew 3:13–15).

John criticized King Herod for marrying his brother's wife, so the king threw John into prison (Luke 3:19–20). Later, at his wife's instigation, Herod had John killed. Jesus said of John, "I tell you the truth: Among those born of women there has not risen anyone greater than John the Baptist" (Matthew 11:11 NIV).

(106) JONAH

A PROPHET SWALLOWED BY A BIG FISH. God told Jonah to go to Nineveh and preach repentance to its wicked people (Jonah 1:1–2). But Jonah didn't want to go. Instead, he ran away.

Jonah boarded a boat headed toward Spain (Jonah 1:3). On the way, a huge storm came up, and even the pagan sailors sensed that God was punishing someone on board. Jonah admitted that he was running from God, and the sailors—at his request—reluctantly threw him overboard (Jonah 1:8–15). God had prepared a giant fish to swallow Jonah (Jonah 1:17), and he sat in the fish's belly for three days and nights. All the while, he prayed to God. Finally, the fish spit Jonah out onto the shore (Jonah 2:10).

After that, Jonah obeyed God, going to Nineveh to preach. The Ninevites changed their ways, and God was pleased (Jonah 3). Strangely, though, the book ends with Jonah pouting, as he had hoped for the destruction of the wicked city. But God showed His heart for all people in the final words of the book: "Nineveh has more than a hundred and twenty thousand people who cannot tell their right hand from their left, and many cattle as well. Should I not be concerned about that great city?" (Jonah 4:11 NIV).

107 JORDAN RIVER

THE LARGEST AND MOST IMPORTANT RIVER IN ISRAEL. The Jordan River starts in Syria and flows about two hundred miles south through the Sea of Galilee to the northern end of the Dead Sea. The river and the land around it are mentioned often in the Bible—about two hundred times. This is where the Israelites crossed into the Promised Land (Joshua 3:15–17). It is also where John the Baptist preached and baptized people. The river is best known as the place where John baptized Jesus (Matthew 3:13–17).

①⓪⑧ JOSEPH

A NAME SHARED BY SEVERAL MEN IN THE
BIBLE. Four were notable: One was
married to Jesus' mother, Mary. He served
as Jesus' adoptive dad, since Jesus' birth
father was God Himself (Matthew 1:20–
25). Another Joseph, the son of the Old
Testament patriarch Jacob, was sold as a slave
(Genesis 37:12–36), but later became an
important leader in the Egyptian pharaoh's
kingdom. The third Joseph was a man from
Arimathea. Jesus was buried in this Joseph's
tomb (Matthew 27:57–61). Another Joseph
almost became the twelfth disciple to replace
the wicked Judas Iscariot. But the job went
to another man, named Matthias (Acts
1:23–26).

⓵⓪⓽ JOSHUA

Moses' successor as leader of the
Israelites. Joshua led God's people
into the Promised Land (Joshua 1:1–6) after
overrunning the walled city of Jericho. God
gave Joshua an unusual plan for capturing the
city: Joshua and his army marched around the
perimeter for six days. Then, on the seventh
day, they blew trumpets and shouted, and the
walls came crashing down (Joshua 6:1–20).
Joshua was a strong leader who seemed to do
everything right—the Bible never records a
sinful episode with him. He died at age 110
(Joshua 24:29).

110 JUDAH

THE SOUTHERN JEWISH KINGDOM. **When King Solomon died, the Israelites split into two kingdoms. The northern kingdom kept the name Israel. The southern kingdom, called Judah, had its capital at Jerusalem (1 Kings 14:21). At many times in their history, the people of Judah worshipped idols and otherwise disrespected God. So He allowed the Babylonian army to destroy Jerusalem. Babylon took the people away and made them slaves; though, years later, some of the people came back to rebuild the city (2 Chronicles 36:20–23).**

111 JUDAS ISCARIOT

THE DISCIPLE WHO BETRAYED JESUS. **He seemed trustworthy—in fact, he was keeper of the disciples' money (John 13:29). But Judas was the one who betrayed Jesus to the high priests and elders for thirty silver coins (Matthew 26:14–15). After Jesus was arrested, Judas felt remorse and tried to give the money back. But the religious leaders refused, and Judas decided to kill himself. The place where he died is called the Field of Blood (Matthew 27:1–10).**

112 JUDGMENT, LAST

THE DAY WHEN GOD SEPARATES THE SAVED FROM THE LOST. At the end of time, Jesus will return to gather all His people and take them away to heaven. Everyone who does not believe will be judged (Matthew 25:31–33). Though it will be a wonderful day for those who believe, it will be terrible for nonbelievers (Romans 2:5–8). No one knows exactly when Jesus will return, so the Bible says to be prepared (1 Thessalonians 5:1–11).

113 JUSTIFICATION

BEING MADE RIGHT WITH GOD. Humans can't be right with God by their own accomplishments or good works. We are only justified by believing in Jesus Christ (Romans 4:25). When we are right with God, we are at peace with Him—and we have the hope of living with Him in heaven (Titus 3:5–7).

❶❶❹ KINGDOM OF GOD

THE RULE OF GOD IN CHRISTIANS' HEARTS (LUKE 17:20–21). Jesus preached what Mark called "the gospel of the kingdom of God" (Mark 1:14). Jesus taught His disciples to seek God's kingdom (Matthew 6:33) and pray for it to come to earth (Matthew 6:10).

❶❶❺ LAMB OF GOD

A NAME USED FOR CHRIST. In Bible times, lambs were often used for sacrifices. This name fits Jesus well because His death was a sacrifice for sins. The prophet Isaiah compared Jesus' death to the death of a lamb: "He was silent like a lamb being led to the butcher, as quiet as a sheep having its wool cut off" (Isaiah 53:7 CEV). When John the Baptist saw Jesus, he said, "Here is the Lamb of God who takes away the sin of the world!" (John 1:29 CEV). In heaven, Jesus is praised as the Lamb of God (Revelation 5:12–13).

116 LAZARUS

MARY AND MARTHA'S BROTHER. When Jesus heard that Lazarus was sick, He said, "His sickness won't end in death. It will bring glory to God and his Son" (John 11:4 CEV). After Lazarus died, Jesus brought him back to life, and many who saw the miracle put their faith in Christ. Others were angry, though, the Jewish leaders making plans to kill Jesus (John 11:41–53). They planned to kill Lazarus, too, blaming him for making so many people put their faith in Jesus (John 12:10–11).

117 LEPROSY

SKIN DISEASES. Those with leprosy were called *lepers*, and in Bible times, people feared them. Lepers had to follow special rules, including living apart from others. They also had to shout, "Unclean!" wherever they went so non-lepers could stay away from them (Leviticus 13:45–46). But Jesus was kind to lepers, as He was to many of the sick and possessed. Once, ten lepers asked for Jesus' help and He healed them all (Luke 17:11–14). Jesus gave His disciples the power to heal (Matthew 10:1), and specifically mentioned cleansing lepers (Matthew 10:8).

⓵⓵⓼ Lord's Day

SUNDAY, THE FIRST DAY OF THE WEEK. The Lord's day (Revelation 1:10) is also the day that most Christians worship God in churches. People of the Jewish faith worship on Saturday, the last day of the week, called the Sabbath. After Jesus rose from the dead on the first day of the week, Christians made Sunday their normal day for worship (Acts 20:7). In AD 321, the Roman emperor Constantine made it a Christian holiday.

⓵⓵⓽ Lot

ABRAHAM'S NEPHEW. Lot went with his uncle Abraham to Canaan (Genesis 12:5). Abraham let Lot choose where to live in Canaan, and Lot picked the lush Jordan Valley (Genesis 13:10–11). Unfortunately, that was near the wicked city of Sodom. In time, God decided to destroy Sodom for its sins, but He sent an angel to save Lot's family. The angel told them to run and not look back. Lot and his two daughters escaped, but his wife didn't—she looked back and was turned into a pillar of salt. Read more in Genesis 19:15–26.

❶❷⓿ LUKE

A CHRISTIAN DOCTOR (COLOSSIANS 4:14) AND AUTHOR OF TWO NEW TESTAMENT BOOKS. Luke wrote the third and longest Gospel and the book of Acts. Born a Gentile (which means his family was not Jewish), he also went with Paul on some of his missionary trips (Acts 16:10). Luke was the last to stay with Paul before he died (2 Timothy 4:11).

❶❷❶ LYDIA

A BUSINESSWOMAN OF THE BIBLE. Lydia lived in the city of Thyatira where she sold purple cloth. After Lydia heard Paul preach in Philippi, she and her household were baptized and became Christians. She asked Paul and his friends to stay at her home (Acts 16:14–15).

①②② MANNA

MIRACLE FOOD. God gave the Israelites manna when they were in the wilderness. In Hebrew, the word *manna* means, "What is it?" In the Bible, it's called "bread from heaven" (Exodus 16:4), and described as tiny white seeds that "tasted like something baked with sweet olive oil" (Numbers 11:8 CEV). The people would grind or crush the seeds into flour. Then they would "boil it and make it into thin wafers" (Numbers 11:9 CEV).

❶❷❸ MARK

A COUSIN OF BARNABAS (COLOSSIANS 4:10).
Mark went with Barnabas and Paul on
the first mission trip (Acts 12:25). Mark went
as far as Perga, then turned back to Jerusalem
(Acts 13:3–13). Because of Mark's vacillation,
Paul wouldn't let him go on the next trip.
Barnabas, who wanted to take Mark, parted
ways with Paul (Acts 15:36–41). Mark's
mother was a Christian woman named Mary,
and people who followed the Lord went
to her home to pray (Acts 12:12). Mark
is believed to be the author of the second
Gospel.

①②④ MARY

A NAME SHARED BY MANY WOMEN IN THE
BIBLE. The most well known are Jesus'
mother and Mary Magdalene. Jesus' mother,
often called "the Virgin Mary," was engaged
to Joseph. An angel told her she would give
birth to Jesus (Luke 1:26–35). She followed
her son's ministry through the years, and
witnessed His crucifixion, when Jesus put
her into the care of His disciple John (John
19:26–27). Mary Magdalene, the other Mary,
also saw Jesus being crucified (Matthew
27:55–61). When she saw His empty tomb,
she told the disciples (John 20:1–2). This
Mary was one of the first to see Jesus after
He'd risen from the dead (Mark 16:9). A
third Mary was the sister of Martha and
Lazarus. She listened to Jesus' teaching while
her sister busied herself with hostessing
(Luke 10:38–39). Mary once poured perfume
on Jesus' feet and wiped them with her hair
(John 12:1–3).

❶❷❺ MATTHEW

A TAX COLLECTOR WHO BECAME ONE OF
JESUS' TWELVE DISCIPLES (MATTHEW
9:9). He wrote the first book in the New
Testament, a job made easier by his
unpopular career choice. Those who collected
taxes had to be good at keeping records,
and that made Matthew a good choice for a
writer. Some people called Matthew "Levi"
(Mark 2:13–17; Luke 5:27–32). The proud
Pharisees lumped Matthew (a "publican")
with other "sinners" that Jesus ate with
(Matthew 9:11).

❶❷❻ MELCHIZEDEK

A N ANCIENT KING AND PRIEST. Abraham
gave Melchizedek a tenth of all he had
(Genesis 14:18–20). A mysterious figure, we
don't know about Melchizedek's parents or
his death (Hebrews 7:3), but the Bible says
his priesthood is endless (Hebrews 7:16).
In the book of Psalms, King David said the
Messiah would be a priest forever, just like
this king (Psalm 110:4).

❶❷❼ MERCY SEAT

T HE LID OF THE ARK OF THE COVENANT
(EXODUS 25:17–21). It was made out of
pure gold, with two carved angels facing each
other. The Lord told Moses, "I will meet you
there between the two creatures and tell you
what my people must do and what they must
not do" (Exodus 25:22 CEV). Once a year, the
high priest sprinkled blood from a sacrificed
bull and goat on the seat. This was done for
his sins and the sins of the people (Leviticus
16:11–16).

❶❷❽ METHUSELAH

A SON OF ENOCH (GENESIS 5:21) AND
NOAH'S GRANDFATHER. He lived to be
969 years old (Genesis 5:27), the longest life
span recorded in the Bible.

①②⑨ MIRACLE

A N ACT OF GOD THAT GOES AGAINST THE
LAWS OF NATURE. In the New Testament,
miracles are called signs, wonders, mighty
works, and powers. Most miracles took place
in one of five biblical periods. The first period
was the Exodus (Exodus 7, 9, 10, 14). The
next was during the lives of Elijah (1 Kings
18:30–39) and Elisha (2 Kings 4:2–7). The
third period was during the Exile (Daniel
3:9–27). The fourth was Jesus' time—His
miracles were signs that He possessed God's
power (Matthew 15:33–39) to heal the sick
(Matthew 8:14–17), give life to the dead
(Matthew 9:23–25), even calm the wind and
sea (Luke 8:22–25). The fifth period was the
time of the apostles' work. Their miracles
proved they were disciples of Jesus (Acts
3:6–9).

❶❸⓿ MOSES

A PROPHET OF ISRAEL WHO WROTE THE FIRST FIVE BOOKS OF THE BIBLE. Moses was a Hebrew, born in Egypt during the Israelites' years of slavery there. He spent the first forty years of his life in Egypt, after escaping the Pharaoh's order that all the Hebrew boy babies should be killed (Exodus 1:16). Moses' mother put him in a basket along the Nile River, where the king's daughter found and adopted him. Read more in Exodus 2:1–10. Years later, after killing an Egyptian who was mistreating a Hebrew slave, Moses ran away into the desert (Exodus 2:12–15).

Moses spent the next forty years in Midian, married a woman named Zipporah, and had two sons (Exodus 18:2–4). God called Moses to go back to Egypt to lead the Israelites out of slavery (Exodus 3:11–4:20). God sent ten plagues on Egypt to convince the Pharaoh to let Moses and the people leave. Moses then led the people into the Sinai Peninsula.

The last forty years of Moses' life were spent in this wilderness. God gave Moses the Ten Commandments here (Exodus 20:1–24). Moses built the tabernacle, following God's instructions (Exodus 35–40). At one point, when the Israelites were without water in Kadesh, they grumbled and God told Moses to speak to a large rock to cause water to come from it. Moses, frustrated with the people, hit the rock with his staff. Though water still gushed from the rock (Numbers 20:2–11), God was angry with Moses' disobedience and their failure to honor God in front of the others. So God said Moses and Aaron would not be the ones to lead His people into the Promised Land (Numbers 20:12). God let Moses view the Promised Land from Mount Nebo, where he died at age 120 (Deuteronomy 34:1–7).

❶❸❶ MOUNT ARARAT

THE PLACE WHERE NOAH'S ARK LANDED (GENESIS 8:4). Mount Ararat is in modern-day Turkey, and rises higher than any other mountain in its range. Ancient Persians called Ararat "Noah's mountain," though no one knows the exact spot where the ark landed. Some people have searched for its remains on Mount Urartu in eastern Armenia.

❶❸❷ MOUNT OF OLIVES

A HILL BEYOND THE KIDRON VALLEY EAST OF JERUSALEM. Many stories in the Bible took place at the Mount of Olives. Jesus often went to the Mount of Olives (Luke 22:39), and had an important talk with His disciples there (Matthew 24:3–26:2). This is where Judas betrayed Jesus the night before He was crucified (Matthew 26:30, 47). It's also where Jesus talked to the disciples after He rose from the dead (Acts 1:1–12). In Old Testament times, the branches of olive trees from this place were used to make booths for a special feast (Nehemiah 8:15).

❶❸❸ NAZARETH

J ESUS' BOYHOOD HOMETOWN. **Nazareth**
is a village in Galilee near the Plain of
Esdraelon. Mount Carmel is fifteen miles to
the northwest. Nazareth is where Mary was
when the angel told her she was going to give
birth to Jesus (Luke 1:26–38). Mary, Joseph,
and Jesus came back here after they had run
away to Egypt (Matthew 2:20–23). Nazareth
was where Jesus lived as a boy, gaining the
name "Jesus of Nazareth" (Mark 1:24). The
people of Nazareth were often offended by
things Jesus said, and one time they tried to
throw Him off a cliff (Luke 4:16–30)!

❶❸❹ NEBUCHADNEZZAR

APOWERFUL KING OF BABYLONIA.
Nebuchadnezzar's father began the Chaldean
Empire, and Nebuchadnezzar was in charge of
his army. Nebuchadnezzar became king upon
his father's death. As king, Nebuchadnezzar
attacked Jerusalem and his soldiers took things
made of gold, silver, and bronze from the temple.
They burned the temple and took many people
of Judah into exile. God allowed the devastation
as punishment for Judah's sins (2 Chronicles
36:15–20).

𝟭𝟯𝟱 New Covenant

G OD'S FINAL PROMISE OR AGREEMENT WITH
HIS PEOPLE. The prophet Jeremiah
predicted this new agreement (Jeremiah
31:31–34), and Jesus' Passover meal with His
disciples was a symbol of it. Jesus called the
cup the "new covenant in my blood" (Luke
22:20 NIV). Christ is the one who makes this
new and better agreement possible. "Christ
died to rescue those who had sinned and
broken the old agreement. Now he brings
his chosen ones a new agreement with
its guarantee of God's eternal blessings!"
(Hebrews 9:15 CEV).

❶❸❻ NICODEMUS

A PHARISEE WHO KNEW JESUS WAS THE
MESSIAH. Nicodemus talked with Jesus
about the new birth, when Jesus told him a
person must be saved—born of the Spirit—
before he or she can get into God's kingdom
(John 3:1–7). Nicodemus bravely warned
the Jewish leaders not to judge Jesus before
hearing what He had to say (John 7:50–51).
Later, Nicodemus helped prepare Jesus' body
for burial (John 19:39–42).

➊➌➐ NOAH

THE ARK BUILDER. Noah was chosen by God to save life on earth by building a huge wooden boat to escape the great flood. Noah was the son of Lamech and the father of Shem, Ham, and Japheth. After he built the ark, the six-hundred-year-old Noah went inside with his family and each type of animal (Genesis 7:6–9). Then God sent rain that lasted forty days and nights—coupled with the "fountains of the great deep" (Genesis 7:11), water flooded the entire earth. When the flood ended, Noah's family and the animals left the ark. Noah built an altar to worship God (Genesis 8:20), and the Lord made a covenant, or promise, with Noah (Genesis 9:1–17), saying He would never again punish the entire earth by water. Noah died at the age of 950 (Genesis 9:29).

❶❸❽ OMNIPOTENCE

G OD'S GREAT POWER. There are no limits
to God's power. He controls nature
(Amos 4:13). He also controls what happens
to all nations (Amos 1–2).

❶❸❾ OMNIPRESENCE

G OD'S GREAT PRESENCE. God is in all
places at all times. No one can hide
from Him (Jeremiah 23:23–24). God's Spirit
is with us in all we do (John 14:3, 18).

❶❹⓿ OMNISCIENCE

G OD'S GREAT KNOWLEDGE. God is very
wise and He knows all. Christ is the key
to understanding all of God's wisdom and
knowledge (Colossians 2:2–3).

141 PALESTINE

THE HOLY LAND. The name *Palestine* came from a Greek word that means "land of the Philistines." The giant warrior Goliath, felled by David, was a Philistine. Three great world religions came out of Palestine: Judaism, Christianity, and Islam.

142 PARABLE

A STORY THAT TEACHES A LESSON. A parable is like a fable, using comparisons to teach deep truths. Jesus often spoke in parables— His followers could understand them, but unbelievers could not. Examples of parables include:

The Wise and
  Foolish Builders . . . . Matthew 7:24–27
The Lost Sheep . . . . Luke 15:3–7
The Prodigal Son . . . . Luke 15:11–32
The Sower . . . . Matthew 13:3–23

❶❹❸ PASSOVER

A N IMPORTANT JEWISH HOLIDAY. Passover is when Jews remember the Israelites' Exodus from Egypt. The Israelites were slaves in Egypt for many years, until God sent plagues on the country to convince the Pharaoh to let the people go. The last plague was the death of the firstborn of every Egyptian family. To protect the Israelites from this plague, God told His people to paint the blood of a lamb over the doors of their houses. When He came to take the firstborn, He would "pass over" the homes that had blood over the doors (Exodus 12:13). After all the Egyptian firstborn died, Pharaoh let the Israelites go.

144 PAUL

A JESUS-HATER WHO BECAME A CHRISTIAN MISSIONARY. At first, Paul (then known as Saul) was against Christianity. In fact, he wanted to arrest and kill those who taught about Jesus (Acts 9:1). One day, on the road to Damascus, a bright light shone around Saul from heaven. He fell to the ground and heard Jesus' voice: "Saul, Saul, why do you persecute me?" (Acts 9:4 NIV). Jesus told Saul—who had been blinded by the light—to get up and go to Damascus. Saul was without his sight for three days. Then God sent a man named Ananias to heal Saul's eyes. Saul became a strong believer in Jesus, and was soon known as Paul. He took long missionary trips to share the gospel, and wrote many of the books in the New Testament.

❶❹❺ PENTECOST

THE DAY ON WHICH THE HOLY SPIRIT WAS
GIVEN TO BELIEVERS. *Pentecost* comes from
the Greek word *pentekoste*, which means
"fiftieth." In the Old Testament, Pentecost
was a harvest festival (the Feast of Harvest,
Exodus 23:16), celebrated fifty days after the
Passover lamb was killed. In New Testament
times, Pentecost was the day when the Holy
Spirit came to earth to live in Jesus' followers
(Acts 2:1–42). That happened fifty days
after Jesus—known as *the Lamb of God*—was
killed. When the Holy Spirit came, believers
were filled with great joy, and Jesus' disciples
worked many miracles. The church grew
rapidly.

❶❹❻ PERSECUTION

OPPRESSION FOR ONE'S BELIEFS. Jesus was persecuted because He said He was the Son of God. His followers were persecuted for believing in Him. Jesus said that when believers are persecuted, God will bless them (Matthew 5:10). He also taught that we should pray for people who persecute us (Matthew 5:44). Faith in God helps us to handle persecution (Ephesians 6:16).

❶❹❼ PERSIA

A GREAT NATION OF OLD TESTAMENT TIMES. Persia was a country covering most of the same territory as modern day Iran. The Persians conquered Babylon in 539 BC. Then they began to allow the Israelites to leave their captivity (2 Chronicles 36:20–23). The Persian king Artaxerxes let Nehemiah go back to Jerusalem to rebuild the city wall (Nehemiah 2:1–8). Alexander the Great defeated the Persians around 330 BC.

❶❹❽ PETER

ONE OF JESUS' CLOSEST FRIENDS. Also
known as Simon, Peter was one of
Jesus' twelve disciples, called away from his
job as a fisherman. Peter was daring and
impetuous, the disciple who cut off a man's
ear when he came to arrest Jesus (John
18:10). Jesus scolded Peter and healed the
man. When Peter saw Jesus walking on water,
he asked to join Jesus and walked on the
water—briefly—as well (Matthew 14:25–32).
Before Jesus was arrested, Peter promised that
he would be forever loyal; but when Jesus was
taken away, Peter denied that he'd ever known
Him. In the end, Jesus forgave Peter, and
Peter did stay true to his Lord. Peter was one
of the first two disciples to discover that Jesus
had risen from the dead (John 20:1–10).

❶❹❾ PHARISEES

A POWERFUL GROUP OF JEWISH LEADERS. In Jesus' time, the Pharisees were somewhat like a political party, concerned with the laws of the land. The Pharisees stayed true to the oldest laws and traditions of Israel. But Jesus disagreed with their perspective, emphasizing rules over more important things, like justice, mercy, and love. (See Matthew 23:1–7.) The Pharisees picked apart Jesus' words and actions, accusing Him of breaking the law. For example, the Pharisees were very unhappy when Jesus "worked" by healing a man on the Sabbath (Luke 6:6–11).

❶❺⓿ PHILIP

A NAME SHARED BY ONE OF THE DISCIPLES AND AN EARLY CHURCH LEADER. Jesus invited the first Philip to follow Him, and Philip brought along a friend named Nathanael (John 1:43–51). Both men became Jesus' disciples. This Philip once brought a group of Gentiles to see Jesus when He was in Jerusalem (John 12:20–22). The other Philip was chosen to help the twelve apostles in the church at Jerusalem (Acts 6:1–7). He was said to be honest, wise, and "full of the Holy Ghost" (Acts 6:3).

❶❺❶ PILATE, PONTIUS

A ROMAN GOVERNOR OF JUDEA. Pilate supervised Jesus' trial, though he didn't want to be responsible for Jesus' crucifixion (John 18:28–38). At one point, Pilate sent Jesus to another ruler, Herod, for sentencing. But Herod sent Him back to Pilate (Luke 23:11). The trial took place at Passover time, and each year at Passover, a criminal was set free. Pilate suggested Jesus be released, but the jealous religious leaders stirred the people to call for a prisoner named Barabbas. Pilate ultimately turned Jesus over to be killed, but tried to avoid responsibility by symbolically washing his hands of the case (Matthew 27:24).

❶❺❷ PILLAR OF FIRE AND CLOUD

S IGNS OF GOD'S PRESENCE FOR THE ISRAELITES. When the people were traveling in the wilderness, God gave them signs that He was with them (Numbers 14:13–14). In the daytime, He was in a giant cloud to guide the people on their way. At night, He was in a tall pillar of fire (Exodus 13:21).

❶❺❸ PLAGUE

A DISASTER. God sent ten plagues on Egypt because its leader wouldn't let the Israelites under Moses leave the country (Exodus 7–11). The plagues were:

1. Water turned into blood (Exodus 7:14–25)
2. Frogs everywhere (Exodus 8:1–15)
3. Lice on everything (Exodus 8:16–19)
4. Swarms of flies (Exodus 8:20–32)
5. Disease on farm animals (Exodus 9:1–7)
6. Boils and sores on humans (Exodus 9:8–12)
7. Destructive hail (Exodus 9:13–35)
8. Swarms of locusts (Exodus 10:1–20)
9. Utter darkness for three days (Exodus 10:21–29)
10. Death of firstborn children (Exodus 11:1–12:36)

The first nine plagues weren't enough to convince the Egyptian pharaoh to let the Israelites go. But when his own son died in the tenth plague, he urged Moses and the people to leave.

❶❺❹ PRAYER

TALKING TO GOD. God is so powerful that He can talk—and listen—to everyone at once. In prayer, we can ask God to help us and others (Ephesians 6:18). We can request the things we need (Luke 11:3). We can tell God that we're sorry for our sins (1 John 1:9). We can even pray to God when we just need someone to talk to. After we talk to God, we can take time to listen for what He might be saying to us.

❶❺❺ PRODIGAL SON

THE MAIN CHARACTER IN ONE OF JESUS' PARABLES. Jesus told the story of a young man whose father gave him a lot of money. The young man took the money and went off in search of pleasure. He spent the money foolishly until there was nothing left. By then, he was poor and starving. Not knowing what else to do, the man decided to go home to apologize and offer himself as a servant to his father. But when the older man saw him coming, he was filled with joy. The father put on a huge welcome-home party, picturing God the Father's pleasure when sinful people come to Him. Read more in Luke 15:11–32.

❶❺❻ PUBLICAN

A TAX COLLECTOR. Tax collectors collected money for the Roman government. Matthew was a publican (Matthew 9:9–11). So was Zacchaeus (Luke 19:1–10).

❶❺❼ RABBI

A TITLE OF RESPECT MEANING "MASTER" OR "TEACHER." Mary Magdalene called Jesus "Rabboni" when He appeared to her after rising from His tomb (John 20:16). *Rabboni* is the Aramaic form of *Rabbi*. Nicodemus also used this name for Jesus, saying, "Rabbi, we know you are a teacher who has come from God" (John 3:2 NIV). The disciples of Jesus called Him "Rabbi," too (John 1:38). This title was also used for John the Baptist by his followers (John 3:26). This word is still used in the Jewish faith today for leaders of the congregation and those who teach Jewish law.

❶❺❽ RAINBOW

AN ARCH OF COLORS IN THE SKY. A rainbow appeared after the great flood, a sign from God that He would never destroy the earth with water again (Genesis 9:9–17).

❶❺❾ RAPTURE, THE

A CONCEPT OF CHRIST'S RETURN TO EARTH. Many believe that when Jesus comes back, the redeemed will be changed, gaining glorified bodies like Christ's (Philippians 3:20–21) as they're taken up into the clouds to meet the Lord. The "dead in Christ" will also be raised at that time (1 Thessalonians 4:16–17).

🅰🄺🄾 RED SEA

A BODY OF WATER BETWEEN EGYPT AND ARABIA. God split the Red Sea in two when Moses led the Israelites out of Egypt. God told Moses to hold his walking stick over the sea and a miracle occurred—the people of Israel walked across the sea on dry land, with water on both sides. The Egyptian army, pursuing the Israelites, went into the middle of the water; but the sea came back together, drowning every soldier. Read more in Exodus 14.

🄺🄺🄺 RESURRECTION

R ISING FROM THE DEAD. For believers, resurrection leads to eternal life. Jesus taught His followers to believe in the resurrection, saying, "My Father wants everyone who sees the Son to have faith in him and to have eternal life. Then I will raise them to life on the last day" (John 6:40 CEV). Paul also taught that Jesus would give Christians life that lasts forever (Romans 2:7)—and Jesus provided proof when He Himself rose to life after the crucifixion.

1️⃣6️⃣2️⃣ RUTH

A WOMAN OF GREAT LOYALTY. The brief Old Testament book of Ruth tells her story. She was from Moab, but married a son of the Israelite Naomi. Later, Naomi's husband and both sons died. Naomi wanted to go home to Judea, and loyal Ruth moved with her to Bethlehem (Ruth 1:16–19). There, Ruth worked in the fields owned by a man named Boaz. He was related to Naomi, and ultimately married Ruth. Their descendants included King David and ultimately Jesus (Ruth 4:9–22; Matthew 1:1–6).

🅰🅱🅲 SABBATH

SATURDAY, THE SEVENTH DAY OF THE
WEEK. The Sabbath is the Jewish day of
worship, a symbol of the day God rested
after His creation (Genesis 2:2). Most
Christians worship on the first day of the
week—Sunday. Sunday (1 Corinthians 16:2)
is the day Jesus rose from the dead. One
of the Ten Commandments says that the
Sabbath is a special day that should be kept
holy (Exodus 20:8). Jesus was criticized for
not keeping the Old Testament Sabbath rules
(Matthew 12:1–14). He responded by saying
the Sabbath was made for man, not man for
the Sabbath (Mark 2:27).

❶❻❹ SALT

A SEASONING. Salt is a mineral used to season and preserve food. Jesus called His followers "the salt of the earth" (Matthew 5:13), meaning they should flavor and benefit the world around them. Jesus warned about Christians losing their saltiness (Luke 14:34). If salt loses its flavor, it isn't good for anything—and if a believer loses his purity, neither is he.

❶❻❺ SALVATION

G OD'S WORK OF DELIVERING HUMANS FROM SIN. Salvation is available to everyone, but it's only possible by believing in Jesus Christ (Romans 8:9; Hebrews 5:9). Jesus' death made it possible for anyone to live in heaven with God someday (John 3:36). This salvation protects us from the punishment of hell: "For God hath not appointed us to wrath, but to obtain salvation by our Lord Jesus Christ" (1 Thessalonians 5:9 KJV).

①⑥⑥ SAMARIA

IN BIBLE TIMES, BOTH A REGION AND A CITY. Samaria was the main city of the northern kingdom of Israel. Omri, a king of Israel, built the city in about 900 BC. Samaria was also the name of the whole area around that city. The Assyrians took over Samaria (2 Kings 17:24) around 722 BC, and mixed the Jewish people there with other cultures. The "Samaritans," as the mixed people were called, were hated by the Jews. Jesus, however, showed compassion for Samaritans, healing a man of leprosy in Samaria (Luke 17:11–19) and talking with a Samaritan woman at a well (John 4:1–30). Today, Samaria is part of an area called the West Bank.

167 SAMUEL

THE LAST JUDGE OF ISRAEL (1 SAMUEL 7:15–17). Samuel was also a prophet (1 Samuel 3:19–20). As a little boy, he was taken to the tabernacle to learn from a priest named Eli (1 Samuel 1:23–2:11). As a man, he became the Israelites' leader. Samuel led the people in worshipping God, and oversaw a long period of peace. When Samuel was old, he anointed Saul as Israel's first king (1 Samuel 10:20–24). After Saul disobeyed God, Samuel anointed David the new king (1 Samuel 16:13). Upon Samuel's death, he was given a huge funeral: "People from all over Israel gathered to mourn for him" (1 Samuel 25:1 CEV).

❶❻❽ SARAH

ABRAHAM'S WIFE (GENESIS 11:29) AND MOTHER OF ISAAC. Sarah was also called *Sarai*. She was more than ninety years old when Isaac was born. Her husband was one hundred years old (Genesis 17:17)! God said that He would bless Sarah, that she would become "a mother of nations" (Genesis 17:16). She was an ancestor to all the Israelites, kings, and even to Jesus. Sarah was 127 years old when she died. Her supposed burial site, called the Tomb of the Patriarchs, is a popular tourist site near Hebron, about twenty miles from Jerusalem.

❶❻❾ SATAN

ANOTHER NAME FOR THE DEVIL. Jesus called Satan "the father of lies" (John 8:44). His work goes as far back as the Garden of Eden, where, as a serpent, he tempted Eve to eat the forbidden fruit (Genesis 3:1–6). Jesus also called Satan "the prince of this world" (John 16:11), but his power is limited to what God allows him. In the end, Satan will be cast into the lake of fire forever (Revelation 20:10).

❶❼⓿ SEA OF GALILEE

A LAKE IN THE NORTHERN PART OF ISRAEL. A freshwater lake about fourteen miles long and seven miles wide, the Sea of Galilee is a popular place for fishermen. Several of Jesus' disciples—James, John, Peter, and Andrew—fished there (Mark 1:16–20). Jesus spent a lot of time near this sea. Once, during a bad storm, He and his disciples were in a boat tossed by the waves. Jesus told the water to calm down, and it did (Matthew 8:23–27). Jesus also walked on water in the Sea of Galilee (John 6:16–20).

❶❼❶ SECOND COMING

J ESUS' RETURN TO EARTH. Before Jesus ascended to heaven He said He would come back—and without any warning. He urged Christians to be prepared (Matthew 24:42). When Jesus comes, He will raise the dead (1 Thessalonians 4:16) and take believers with Him into the air. The Second Coming also starts a chain of events that bring the end of life as we know it. Jesus will punish wicked people who won't believe in Him.

❶❼❷ SENNACHERIB

An Assyrian king. He captured all the cities in Judah except Jerusalem, but extracted tribute money from King Hezekiah (2 Kings 18:13–16). King Sennacherib died as he worshipped a false god (2 Kings 19:36–37). His own sons killed him.

❶❼❸ SERMON ON THE MOUNT

Wide-ranging teachings of Jesus. Large crowds followed Jesus wherever He went, and one time He preached to them from a hillside near Capernaum. Jesus told the people how to find happiness (Matthew 5:3–12), encouraged them to speak up about God (Matthew 5:13–16), reminded them about God's commandments (Matthew 5:17–48), and said they should give to the needy (Matthew 6:1–4). Jesus taught them the Lord's Prayer (Matthew 6:9–13) and other rules about prayer and fasting (Matthew 6:14–18), and told them not to love money more than God (Matthew 6:19–24). He even told the people how to be free from worry (Matthew 6:25–34). Jesus ended His sermon with a parable about obeying God's Word (Matthew 7:24–27).

174 SHEKINAH

GOD'S VISIBLE GLORY. The Bible tells of
God appearing in a cloud, fire, and a
bright light. When the Israelites left Egypt,
God led them in a cloud and a column of fire
(Exodus 13:20–22). God talked to Moses
through a burning bush (Exodus 3). On
the night Jesus was born, the glory of God
showed as a very bright light that frightened
shepherds in the fields (Luke 2:9).

175 SHILOH

ISRAEL'S FIRST CAPITAL CITY. The tabernacle
was located here, and inside the tabernacle,
the ark of the covenant. Over time, the
Israelites became careless with God. Once,
in a battle with the Philistines, the Israelites
took the ark from Shiloh onto the battlefield
as a sort of good luck charm. It didn't work—
the Philistines captured the ark (1 Samuel
4:3–11).

❶❼❻ SIN

T HE BAD THINGS THAT PEOPLE DO. Sin is
disobedience toward God, which began
with Adam and Eve in the Garden of Eden.
From that point on, everyone has sinned
(Romans 5:12–14). Sin is not only our behavior
toward God; it's also how we treat others and
ourselves. Nobody can be perfect before God,
so He sent Jesus to die on the cross and take
the punishment for our sins (Romans 5:8).
Without Jesus, no one would be good enough
to get into heaven (Romans 3:10).

❶❼❼ SODOM AND GOMORRAH

Wicked cities in the time of Abraham (Genesis 14:1–3). The people of Sodom and Gomorrah were perverse and violent. A righteous man named Lot was troubled by the behavior of his neighbors (2 Peter 2:7), and God sent two angels to warn him of the approaching destruction of the cities. Lot took his wife and two daughters by the hand and started running. An angel said, "Run for your lives! Don't even look back. And don't stop in the valley. Run to the hills, where you will be safe" (Genesis 19:17 CEV). But Lot's wife looked back and turned into a block of salt. Then God destroyed Sodom and Gomorrah with fire and brimstone (Genesis 19:23–29).

178 SOLOMON

A WISE KING, SON OF KING DAVID. Solomon followed David as a king of Israel. When God offered the new king anything he wished, Solomon prayed that God would give him wisdom (1 Kings 3). He became famous for his wisdom and his wealth (1 Kings 4:20–34); and at God's command, Solomon built a temple at Jerusalem (1 Kings 5–8). Later, though, Solomon drifted away from God after he married wives who worshipped idols (1 Kings 11:1–8). Solomon put heavy taxes on his people (1 Kings 12:4); and after he died, many rebelled against his son Rehoboam and the nation was divided. The rebels formed the northern kingdom of Israel, where Solomon's servant, Jeroboam, ruled. Rehoboam ruled the southern kingdom of Judah. Read more in 1 Kings 12:1–19.

🅐🅐🅐 SPIRITUAL GIFTS

SPECIAL ABILITIES GIVEN TO BELIEVERS. The Bible lists many gifts that God's Holy Spirit can give to believers. The greatest of these is love (1 Corinthians 13:13), while other gifts of the Spirit are preaching, serving, teaching, encouraging, giving, leading, and helping (Romans 12:6–8). Wisdom, knowledge, faith, and discernment are also His gifts (1 Corinthians 12:8–11).

🅐🅐🅐 STEPHEN

ONE OF THE FIRST DEACONS OF THE CHRISTIAN CHURCH (ACTS 6:5). Stephen was "a man full of faith and of the Holy Ghost" (Acts 6:5 KJV). His job as deacon was to help Jesus' twelve disciples, allowing them to teach and pray while Stephen and six other men served the physical needs of church members. But God also gave Stephen the gift of performing miracles (Acts 6:8). The Jewish leaders didn't like Stephen's influence with the people (Acts 6:10), and they had him arrested and stoned to death. As he was dying, Stephen said: "Lord Jesus, receive my spirit. . . . Do not hold this sin against them" (Acts 7:59–60 NIV).

181 STONING

AN ANCIENT PUNISHMENT. When a person was stoned, others stood around and threw rocks at that person until he or she died. Godly men were sometimes stoned because of their faith. Stephen was one of them (Acts 7:59).

182 SYNAGOGUE

A JEWISH CHURCH BUILDING. Paul taught about Jesus in synagogues during his missionary journeys (Acts 18:4).

183 TABERNACLE

A PORTABLE WORSHIP CENTER. In early Israel, there was no permanent worship center. The tabernacle was a large tent where people worshipped. God told the Israelites to build His tabernacle in the wilderness, calling it the "Tent of Meeting" (Exodus 40:1–8 NIV). It was specially made to be moved from place to place. Animals were sacrificed to God at the tabernacle (Leviticus 1:1–9), symbols of what was to come. The greatest sacrifice of all—Jesus' death on the cross—ended the need for animal sacrifice (Hebrews 7:27).

❶❽❹ TEMPLE

ISRAEL'S PLACE OF WORSHIP. After the death of King David, the Jewish people worshipped at the temple in Jerusalem. Solomon built the first one, a beautiful structure ninety feet long, thirty feet wide, and forty-five feet high. It had a porch that was thirty feet long and fifteen feet wide (1 Kings 6:3). Some of its walls were covered with gold and decorated with precious stones. The ark of the covenant was kept in the temple. Read more about this temple in 2 Chronicles 3–4. After about 350 years, the Israelites' enemy, the Babylonians, destroyed Solomon's temple. A second temple was built about seventy years after that, under the direction of a man named Zerubbabel. Then a few years before Jesus was born, King Herod the Great began to build a bigger, more impressive temple on the same site. It was destroyed by the Roman army in AD 70.

❶❽❺ TEMPTATION

AN INNER DRAW TOWARD SIN. Everyone has faced temptation, even Jesus. Read how Satan tempted Jesus in Matthew 4:1–11. The Lord's Prayer (Matthew 6:9–13) teaches us to ask God to protect us from temptation. The Bible says God will help us when we are tempted (1 Corinthians 10:13).

❶❽❻ TEN COMMANDMENTS

AN IMPORTANT SEGMENT OF GOD'S LAW.
God gave the Ten Commandments to
Moses (Exodus 20:1–17), telling him to
share them with the people of Israel. The Ten
Commandments are:

1. Have no other gods before God
   (Exodus 20:3).
2. Don't worship idols (Exodus 20:4).
3. Don't use God's name in a disrespectful
   way (Exodus 20:7).
4. Keep the Sabbath as a day to honor God
   (Exodus 20:8).
5. Respect your parents (Exodus 20:12).
6. Don't murder (Exodus 20:13).
7. Don't commit adultery (Exodus 20:14).
8. Don't steal (Exodus 20:15).
9. Don't lie (Exodus 20:16).
10. Don't covet—that is, desire things that
    belong to others (Exodus 20:17).

❶❽❼ THOMAS

THE DOUBTING DISCIPLE. He was also
called *Didymus*, which means "twin"
(John 11:16). Thomas was one of Jesus'
original twelve disciples (Matthew 10:2–4),
best known for doubting the resurrection of
Christ. Thomas demanded proof, saying he
wanted to see the nail marks on Jesus' hands
and the hole in His side where He'd been
stuck with a spear. So Jesus showed him, and
Thomas believed. Jesus told Thomas that he
had believed what he could see. But there is
a special blessing for people who believe God
without seeing proof. Read more in John
20:24–29.

188 TIMOTHY

Paul's young friend, called "my son in the faith" (1 Timothy 1:2). Timothy's father was Greek, and his mother Jewish. He was raised as a Christian by his mother, Eunice, and grandmother, Lois, both women of strong faith (2 Timothy 1:5). Paul and Timothy traveled together and taught others about Jesus, sharing imprisonment in Rome for a while (Hebrews 13:23). Later, Paul wrote two letters to the young man, the New Testament books called 1 and 2 Timothy.

189 TOWER OF BABEL

The birthplace of multiple languages. Not long after the flood, humans banded together to build a tall tower and make a name for themselves. God upset their prideful plans by giving the people different languages so they couldn't understand one another, then scattered them around the world. The name Babel comes from the Hebrew word for "confuse." Read more in Genesis 11:1–9.

❶❾❶ TRANSFIGURATION

A CHANGING. Jesus once took Peter, James, and John up a high mountain where Jesus' appearance changed. His face glowed like the sun and His clothes became like a bright, white light. This "transfiguration" frightened the disciples, who were surprised to see the Old Testament figures Moses and Elijah appear with Jesus. Then God's voice boomed from a cloud, saying, "This is my beloved Son, in whom I am well pleased; hear ye him" (Matthew 17:5 KJV).

❶❾❶ TRINITY, THE

G OD THE FATHER, JESUS THE SON, AND THE HOLY SPIRIT. *Trinity* means "three." The "Godhead" (Colossians 2:9 KJV) is three persons in one:

    1) God, our heavenly Father
        (Ephesians 3:14–15);
    2) Jesus, the Son of God (John 11:27),
        on earth as God in the form of man; and
    3) the Holy Spirit, who convicts (John 16:8)
        and guides (John 16:13–15) people,
        giving believers special talents and
        encouraging them to use those "gifts" for
        God.

❶❾❷ Twelve, the

J esus' original disciples. These were the men Jesus chose personally (John 15:16) to travel with Him and help Him teach. The twelve were Peter, Andrew, James the son of Zebedee, John, Philip, Bartholomew, Thomas, Matthew, James the son of Alphaeus, Thaddaeus, Simon, and Judas Iscariot (Matthew 10:2–4). Jesus allowed the twelve to cast out evil spirits and heal sick people (Matthew 10:1). Most of them apparently suffered martyrdom after the New Testament was written.

❶❾❸ Unleavened Bread

B read made without yeast. Without yeast, bread dough doesn't rise. This "unleavened" bread is flat, and the subject of a Jewish festival. The Feast of the Unleavened Bread celebrates the Israelites' escape from Egypt (Exodus 13:3), recalling how quickly the escaping slaves left the country. The Israelites departed in such a hurry that they had no time to put yeast into their bread mix. Instead, they wrapped the dough in cloth and rushed away (Exodus 12:33–34).

➊➒➍ URIM AND THUMMIM

P RIESTLY OBJECTS FROM OLD TESTAMENT
TIMES. The exact nature of the Urim and
Thummin is a mystery, but they might have
been colored stones or metal. These objects
were in the breastplate of the high priest Aaron
(Exodus 28:30). They may have been cast as
lots to show the will of God (Numbers 27:21).

➊➒➎ VIRGIN BIRTH

H OW JESUS CAME INTO THIS WORLD. An
angel visited Jesus' mother, Mary,
telling her that she would have a very special
baby named Jesus (Luke 1:31–33). But Mary
asked, "How will this be, since I am a virgin?"
(Luke 1:34 NIV). The angel answered, "The
Holy Spirit will come upon you, and the
power of the Most High will overshadow
you. So the holy one to be born will be called
the Son of God" (Luke 1:35 NIV). Being the
Son of God made Jesus holy. But being born
to a human mother made Him like His own
creation. *Immanuel* is a Hebrew word that
means "God is with us." Long before Jesus
was born, the prophet Isaiah predicted this
amazing birth, saying, "The Lord himself will
give you a sign: The virgin will be with child
and will give birth to a son, and will call him
Immanuel" (Isaiah 7:14 NIV).

❶❾❻ WITNESS

A PERSON TELLS WHAT HE OR SHE KNOWS.
A witness gives "testimony," just like in
a court of law. In Bible times, the testimony
of at least two witnesses was needed to find a
person guilty of a capital crime (Deuteronomy
17:6). Anyone who told lies while testifying
was punished (Deuteronomy 19:18–19). As
New Testament believers, we are called to be
witnesses for Christ (Acts 1:8).

❶❾❼ WORSHIP

P RAISING AND ADORING GOD. Worship
can occur at church, but God can be
worshipped anywhere (Deuteronomy 6:5–7).
A person can worship God alone or with
others (Daniel 6:10; Psalm 132:7). In Bible
times, the Jews worshipped in the tabernacle
until they started using the temple. After they
were taken to live among the Babylonians
and Persians, they worshipped in synagogues.
The book of Psalms, essentially the Jewish
hymn book, is full of praise and worship
for God. Psalm 95:6 says, "Bow down and
worship the LORD our Creator!" (CEV).

❶❾❽ YAHWEH

A KEY OLD TESTAMENT NAME FOR GOD.
In Hebrew, Yahweh appears as these
four letters: יהוה . Read the letters
from right to left. In English, it looks like
the four consonants YHWH. Many Bibles
today translate the word *Yahweh* as Lord or
Jehovah.

❶❾❾ ZACCHAEUS

A SHORT TAX COLLECTOR. One day, as Jesus passed through Jericho, crowds came out to see Him. Since Zacchaeus was "little of stature" (Luke 19:3 KJV), he climbed a tree to get a better look at Jesus. When Jesus saw Zacchaeus in the tree, He told him to come down, "for to day I must abide at thy house" (Luke 19:5 KJV). Zacchaeus hurried to Jesus and promised to make amends for any cheating he'd done as a tax collector. Zacchaeus said he would give half of his money to the poor and pay back anyone he had cheated, fourfold. Jesus was pleased with Zacchaeus's choice, saying, "This day is salvation come to this house" (Luke 19:9 KJV).